Andrew Woods

# OXFORD GRAMMAR 3

Name: _____

Class: _____

OXFORD
UNIVERSITY PRESS
AUSTRALIA & NEW ZEALAND

# CONTENTS

OXFORD UNIVERSITY PRESS

## UNIT 1.1  Common nouns

# Just kidding!

Why did the girl throw the butter out of the window?

She wanted to see the butterfly.

What did the grape say when the elephant stepped on it?

Nothing, it just let out a little wine.

Waiter: How did you find the steak, Madam?

Customer: It was easy. It was just between the potato and the carrots.

What sort of shoes do koalas wear?

Gumboots.

What did the tiger say when he saw a rabbit on a skateboard and a goat on a bike?

"Meals on wheels!"

OXFORD UNIVERSITY PRESS

Nouns name things. Common nouns name ordinary things. *Cat, chair, car, field* and *school* are all common nouns. A common noun only begins with a capital letter if it is the first word in a sentence.

**1** Use the clues to write **common nouns** from the jokes.

a   spread me on bread _____

b   an animal with a trunk and big ears _____

c   something to wear on your feet in wet weather _____

d   a drink made from grapes _____

e   an insect _____

f   a female child _____

g   a striped wildcat _____

h   someone who serves you in a restaurant _____

i   a furry animal with a pouch _____

j   something to ride on and pedal _____

k   a round vegetable _____

l   orange root vegetables _____

m   someone who is served in a shop _____

n   a wall opening for light and air _____

o   a small, round fruit _____

Common nouns name everyday things.

**2** Draw lines to match the nouns in Box A with the nouns in Box B to make three **common nouns** from the jokes page.

A   butter   skate   gum

B   board   boots   fly

**TAKE THE CHALLENGE**

On a piece of paper, write 26 common nouns, each beginning with a different letter of the alphabet.

# Miss de Fyre's Amazing More Machine

Remember: Common nouns name ordinary things.
For example: *table, chair, hand, dog, box, baby*
Plural nouns are nouns that name more than one thing. (Plural means more than one.) For example: *tables, chairs, hands, dogs, boxes, babies*
When changing some nouns to plural, we add or change letters.

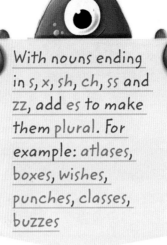

With nouns ending in *s, x, sh, ch, ss* and *zz*, add *es* to make them plural. For example: *atlases, boxes, wishes, punches, classes, buzzes*

When Miss de Fyre puts one thing into her Amazing More Machine, more than one thing comes out the other end.

Miss de Fyre has put one box into her machine and many boxes have come out at the bottom.

To make some plural nouns we just add **s**.
For example: *one girl → many girls     a pencil → a box of pencils     the book → lots of books*

**1** What will come out of Miss de Fyre's machine if she puts her dog into it?

_____

**2** What will come out of Miss de Fyre's machine if she puts in these things?

a   frog _____  b   banana _____  c   flower _____

d   clown _____  e   cup _____  f   apple _____

To make some plural nouns we add **es**.
For example: *one box → many boxes     a bush → lots of bushes     the ditch → three ditches*

**3** Look at these plural nouns for the things that came out of Miss de Fyre's machine next.

a   glasses              b   dishes              c   watches

Write the three things that Miss de Fyre had put into the machine.

a   _____  b   _____  c   _____

**4** Write the plural nouns for the objects that will come out of Miss de Fyre's machine if she puts in these things.

a   fox _____  b   patch _____  c   brush _____

d   dress _____  e   torch _____  f   bus _____

**TAKE THE CHALLENGE**

Write the names of two things you would like to put into Miss de Fyre's machine and the things that would come out.

in _____  out _____  in _____  out _____

# Zoot Galoot – alien visitor

My name is Zoot Galoot.
I come in peace from
the planet Plunk.

This is my
spaceship. It is
called Speedo.

This is my pet
robot. He is
called Cronk.

Now Earthling,
take me to
your weeder.

OXFORD UNIVERSITY PRESS

The names of people, places and things are proper nouns. Proper nouns begin with a capital letter. *Ricky*, *Abdul*, *America*, *Tasmania*, *Friday* and *Grand Final* are all proper nouns.

**1** Read the comic strip about Zoot Galoot. Then answer these questions using proper nouns.

a What is the visiting alien's name? _____

b What is the name of the alien's spaceship? _____

c What is Zoot's robot called? _____

d Where did Zoot come from? _____

> When a proper noun has more than one important word, each word begins with a capital letter. For example: Great Barrier Reef, New Zealand, Mr Clarkson, Melba Highway

**2** a Your teacher's name is a proper noun. Write your teacher's name.

_____

b The name of the town or city in which you live is a proper noun. Write the name of the town or city in which you live. _____

c The name of your school is a proper noun. Write the name of your school. _____

(Did you remember to begin your proper nouns with capital letters?)

Here is Zoot Galoot's computer. ⟶

**3** Zoot Galoot also has a name for his computer. Write a name that you think might suit Zoot's computer. _____

## TAKE THE CHALLENGE

Writers sometimes choose proper nouns that suit the character, so that readers can picture what the character looks like.

a Draw lines to match the characters in Box A with the descriptions in Box B.

b Are the proper nouns in Box A or B? _____

**A**
Sleeping Beauty
The Wiggles
Wonder Woman
Topsy Turvy Tom
Grumpy
Lightning
Tweedledee and Tweedledum
Eeyore (sounds like **heehaw**)

**B**
A pretty but tired princess
An unhappy character
Lively entertainers
A female hero with amazing superpowers
A character who walks on his hands
A fast racehorse
A donkey
Funny twins

# The Noun Show

It's ... The Noun Show ... where you, the audience, get to NAME something!

Now, here's your host ... Davey Dazzle!

Howdy-doody everybody!

I have 12 NOUN cards below.

To be a winner, all you have to do is match the names on each NOUN card with the pictures on the next page!

| | | | |
|---|---|---|---|
| victory | chair | gate | ladder |
| mountain | anger | gossip | fear |
| joy | road | strength | pencil |

Nouns can be concrete or abstract nouns.

Concrete nouns are names for people, places or things that we can see or touch.

For example: *car, man, school, kangaroo*

Abstract nouns name feelings or things we cannot see or touch.

For example: *peace, honesty, love*

**1** Write the concrete nouns on Davey Dazzle's cards under the matching picture.

a

_____

b

_____

c

_____

d

_____

e

_____

f

_____

**2** Write the abstract nouns on Davey Dazzle's cards under the matching picture.

a

_____

b

_____

c

_____

d

_____

e

_____

f

_____

**3** Circle the abstract noun cards on page 10.

**TAKE THE CHALLENGE**

Circle the words that are abstract nouns.

horse        beauty        apple        beach        surprise        sadness

# Black Jack Mack

This is the fearsome and terrible pirate, Black Jack MacDonald.

> I am Black Jack Mack of the Seven Seas, King of the Waves. The oceans are mine.

Black Jack Mack rules the Seven Seas. He is King of the Waves. The oceans are his.

When Black Jack Mack sees a ship laden with treasure, he attacks it and sinks it.

Black Jack Mack captures the sailors on the ship and makes them walk the plank.

> Ha! Ha! Ha! Shark's meat, baby!

Last to be fed to the sharks is Captain Courageous. He trembles with fear. Black Jack Mack you are a cruel pirate!

> Look at the mess you've made, young man!

However, when Mum comes in and pulls the plug on Black Jack Mack, he isn't quite so fearsome or terrible any more.

OXFORD UNIVERSITY PRESS

Pronouns are words that we can use in place of nouns.

For example: *Sam walked **her** dog around the block.* (We use *her* instead of *Sam* again.)

*The bike skidded out of control and **it** crashed into the fence.*

(We use *it* instead of using *the bike* again.)

Here are the pronouns that have been used in the story of Black Jack Mack.

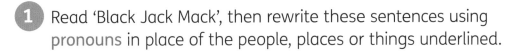

*I    he    mine    his    it    them    she    you*

**1** Read 'Black Jack Mack', then rewrite these sentences using pronouns in place of the people, places or things underlined.

> Using pronouns helps our writing flow because we do not have to repeat the same nouns.

**a** Black Jack Mack rules the Seven Seas. <u>Black Jack Mack</u> is King of the Waves. The oceans are <u>Black Jack Mack's</u>.

_____

_____

**b** When Black Jack Mack sees a ship laden with treasure, <u>Black Jack Mack</u> attacks <u>the ship laden with treasure</u> and sinks <u>the ship laden with treasure</u>.

_____

_____

**c** Black Jack Mack captures the sailors on the ship and makes <u>the sailors</u> walk the plank.

_____

_____

**d** Last to be fed to the sharks is Captain Courageous. <u>Captain Courageous</u> trembles with fear.

_____

_____

**e** When Mum comes in and pulls the plug on Black Jack Mack, <u>Black Jack Mack</u> isn't quite so fearsome or terrible any more.

_____

_____

## TAKE THE CHALLENGE

Choose pronouns from the box that could replace the underlined words.

**a** <u>You and I</u> are walking to school tomorrow. _____

**b** <u>The tiger</u> growled at <u>Emma</u>. _____ _____

**c** <u>Barney</u> threw the ball. _____

| It |
| He |
| We |
| her |

**The Ogs live in the Land of Od.**

# The Ogs of Od

Some Ogs are big. Some Ogs are small.

Some Ogs have long hair.

Some Ogs have short hair.

Some Ogs like soft, soppy music.

Some Ogs like cool dance music.

Most Ogs like loud music.

Some Ogs ride slow, spotty scooters.

Some Ogs drive fast red cars.

All Ogs love to swim in pools filled with thick, mushy, lumpy, green soup!

OXFORD UNIVERSITY PRESS

Some words **describe** or tell us more about nouns.
*He has red hair.  She has an old dog.  Today is wet and cold.*
**a** Which word tells us more about his hair?
**b** Which word tells us more about her dog?
**c** Which words tell us more about today?

Adjectives tell us more about nouns. They can tell us about size, shape, number and colour.

The words *red, old, wet* and *cold* are adjectives.

**1** Read the story about the Ogs of Od and then answer these questions.

   **a** Write the two adjectives in the story that **describe** the size of the Ogs.

   _____ or _____

   **b** Write the two adjectives that **describe** the Ogs' hair.

   _____ or _____

   **c** Write the five adjectives in the story that **describe** the sort of music Ogs like.

   _____ _____ _____ _____ _____

   **d** Write the adjectives that **describe** the sort of scooters some Ogs ride.

   _____

   **e** Write the two adjectives that **describe** the cars that some Ogs drive.

   _____

   **f** Write the adjectives that **describe** the soup in the Ogs' swimming pools.

   _____

**2** Underline the adjectives in these sentences.

   **a** The desert was hot and dusty.

   **b** The three black, savage dogs growled at the tall stranger.

   **c** The funny clown was wearing a purple bow tie and a pointy hat.

   **d** Elly could not fit the six square pegs into the round holes.

## TAKE THE CHALLENGE

Write adjectives from the box that best match the nouns below.

> six    gusty    slippery    untidy    tasty

**a** _____ wind    **b** _____ room

**c** _____ ice    **d** _____ sausages

# DES CRIPTO

She smashes through heavy wooden doors.

Terrible savage monsters cannot stop her.

She crashes through solid brick walls.

She bends and breaks steel gates with her bare hands.

Nothing stops Desiree Cripto when it's home time.

OXFORD UNIVERSITY PRESS

Adjectives help us describe the characters and places in our texts. For example:
*The **quiet**, **thoughful** girl walked along the **windswept**, **deserted** beach.*
Character: *a **quiet**, **thoughful** girl*
Place (also called setting): *a **windswept**, **deserted** beach*

> Adjectives are words that are used to describe nouns. For example: They have bright, yellow coats. (bright and yellow are adjectives)

**1** Write the adjectives from the comic strip that describe these nouns.

a   The doors that Des Cripto smashes down _____

b   The monsters that cannot stop Des Cripto _____

c   The walls that Des Cripto crashes through _____

d   Gates that Des Cripto bends and breaks _____

e   Des Cripto's hands when she bends and breaks gates _____

Some adjectives can be made by adding endings to nouns.
For example:  *wind + y = windy   wonder + ful = wonderful*

**2** Write some of the adjectives from the box next to the characters they best describe. (The adjectives can be used more than once.)

a   monster _____

b   clown _____

c   heroine _____

d   prince _____

> hairy   noble   brave
> funny   royal   scary
> horrible   clever   rich
> handsome   colourful
> bold   bad   clumsy

**3** In the space below, describe the place where one of the characters from question 2 lives. Use as many adjectives as you can in your description. Underline the adjectives.

_____

_____

**TAKE THE CHALLENGE**

Rewrite these nouns. Add **y** or **ful** to make adjectives.

a   rain   _____

b   sand   _____

c   pain   _____

d   mess   _____

e   curl   _____

f   peace   _____

# An anvil for the blacksmith

**Read this alphabet poem with your teacher.**

An anvil for the blacksmith,
A bible for the preacher,
A chisel for a carpenter,
A desktop for the teacher.
An eggflip for the pastry cook,
A frigate for a sailor,
A gateway for the gardener,
And a hemline for the tailor.
An illness for a doctor,
A jetty for an angler,
A keyhole for the locksmith,
A lasso for the wrangler.
A mailbag for the postie,
A novel for a writer,
An opal for the miner and
A punchbag for a fighter.
A queue for the shopper,
A rocket for the flyer,
A songbook for a singer,
A temple for the friar.
An upstairs for the butler,
A volume for a reader,
A whistle for an umpire,
An x-spot for the leader.
A yawn for the poet,
A z or two for snoring,
And when I wake up after lunch,
My rhyme will be less boring.

*The, a* and *an* are called articles. We can use articles before a noun to make a noun group.
For example: **the** blacksmith, **a** jetty, **an** illness

**1** Use the poem to help you write **the**, **a** or **an** before these nouns.

a _____ anvil

b _____ preacher

c _____ chisel

d _____ poet

e _____ illness

f _____ butler

g _____ opal

h _____ tailor

i _____ keyhole

j _____ bible

k _____ eggflip

l _____ teacher

We can add adjectives to make the noun group even more interesting.
For example: *an **angry** teacher, the **long** queue, a **brave** soldier*

**2** Make interesting noun groups below by adding an article and an adjective.

a _____ sailor

b _____ rocket

c _____ apple

d _____ book

e _____ itch

f _____ monster

*The means one particular thing, but a or an shows one of many things. For example: Can you see the boy with blond hair? Can you see a boy with blond hair?*

**3** Use articles to complete these sentences.

a Eight is _____ even number but nine is _____ odd number.

b Maya found _____ egg in _____ hen's nest.

c _____ ant is _____ insect but _____ spider is _____ arachnid.

**TAKE THE CHALLENGE**

Use the article **an** before words beginning with *a, e, i, o, u* (except for some words beginning with *u* and *eu* when *u* and *eu* make a *yoo* sound, which should use the article **a**). All other words begin with the article **a**. Write **a** or **an** before these words.

a _____ European car

b _____ unit

c _____ umpire

d _____ umbrella

e _____ unicorn

f _____ uniform

# Miss Honey's cottage

Miss Honey has invited Matilda back to her little cottage for tea.

They came to a small green gate half-buried in the hedge on the right and almost hidden by the over-hanging hazel branches. Miss Honey paused with one hand on the gate and said, "There it is. That's where I live."

Matilda saw a narrow dirt-path leading to a tiny red-brick cottage. The cottage was so small it looked more like a doll's house than a human dwelling. The bricks it was built of were old and crumbly and very pale red. It had a grey slate roof and one small chimney, and there were two little windows at the front. Each window was no larger than a sheet of tabloid newspaper and there was clearly no upstairs to the place. On either side of the path there was a wilderness of nettles and blackberry thorns and long brown grass. An enormous oak tree stood overshadowing the cottage. Its massive spreading branches seemed to be enfolding and embracing the tiny building, and perhaps hiding it as well from the rest of the world.

from *Matilda* by Roald Dahl

OXFORD UNIVERSITY PRESS

**1** Use the text on page 20 to help you write common nouns to complete the following:

a a small green _____

b a narrow _____

c a grey slate _____

d a tiny _____

**2** Rewrite these nouns as plurals.

a nettle _____    b window _____

c branch _____    d brick _____

Adjectives help to give a clearer picture of the story to the reader.

**3** Use the text on page 20 to write how the author Roald Dahl has used adjectives to help the reader picture Miss Honey's cottage.

a The oak tree was _____.

b Miss Honey's cottage was a _____cottage.

c The cottage had a _____roof.

## TAKE THE CHALLENGE

Rewrite the following sentences using the pronoun **it** where needed.

The cottage was tiny. The cottage was built with bricks that were old and crumbly, and the cottage looked like a doll's house.

_____

_____

_____

_____

_____

# TOPIC 1: TEST YOUR GRAMMAR!

## Nouns, pronouns and adjectives

**1** Shade the bubble next to the common noun.
- ○ think
- ○ Ben
- ○ brain
- ○ laughing

**2** Shade the bubble next to the correct noun plural for **church**.
- ○ churchs
- ○ churches
- ○ churchess
- ○ churchies

**3** Shade the bubble next to the proper noun.
- ○ city
- ○ Hobart
- ○ town
- ○ street

**4** Shade the bubble next to the word that is a concrete noun.
- ○ quick
- ○ school
- ○ thin
- ○ happiness

**5** Shade the bubble next to the abstract noun that completes this sentence.

*After killing the dragon, the warrior was rewarded for her* ⬚ .
- ○ bravely
- ○ bravest
- ○ brave
- ○ bravery

**6** Shade the bubble next to the abstract noun.
- ○ smile
- ○ happiness
- ○ giggle
- ○ chuckle

**7** Shade the bubble next to the noun that would best match a character called Boppo.
- ○ clown
- ○ doctor
- ○ priest
- ○ teacher

**8** Shade the bubble next to the word that best describes these nouns.
*Robert, Australia, Atlantic, July*
- ○ common
- ○ proper
- ○ abstract
- ○ concrete

OXFORD UNIVERSITY PRESS

**9** Shade the bubble next to the word that best describes these nouns.

*rectangle, triangle, pentagon, hexagon*

○ common  ○ proper  ○ abstract  ○ technical

**10** Shade the bubble next to the pronoun from this sentence.

*The bull was so strong that the farmer could not control him.*

○ bull  ○ was  ○ strong  ○ him

**11** Shade the bubble next to the pronoun that would best replace the underlined words in this sentence.

*Lily, Hannah and I are going to the swimming pool today.*

○ They  ○ We  ○ Us  ○ Them

**12** Shade the bubble next to the adjective from this sentence.

*The band was so loud I had to cover my ears.*

○ band  ○ loud  ○ cover  ○ ears

**13** Shade the bubble next to the noun group that uses an incorrect article.

○ the apple  ○ the apples  ○ a apple  ○ an apple

**14** Circle the noun groups in the text below.

*A mighty lion was asleep in the jungle. A cheeky, little mouse climbed onto the lion's*

*back. The lion woke up. The terrified mouse hid behind a large, green fern.*

## HOW AM I DOING?

Colour the boxes if you understand.

Common nouns name ordinary things. ☐

Proper nouns are the names of people, places and things. They begin with a capital letter. ☐

Concrete nouns name things that can be seen or touched. ☐

Abstract nouns name things that cannot be seen or touched. ☐

Adjectives describe nouns. ☐

Pronouns are words that can take the place of nouns. ☐

**UNIT 2.1**   Doing verbs

# The big game - Ogs vs Ugs

The Mighty Ogs ran out onto the field.

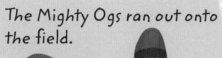

The umpire bounced the ball. Big Toddy Og tapped the ball to tiny Tommy Og.

Tommy sprinted with the ball. He passed to Terri Og.

Terri caught the ball and she kicked it quickly.

The ball landed near Timmy Og. He picked it up.

Timmy dodged and weaved around the Ug defenders.

He booted the ball through the goals. Timmy turned to celebrate.

The Ug players laughed. Oops! Wrong end! Score = Ugs 1 Ogs 0.

Coach Olly Og tears out his hair.

Some words tell us what is happening or what someone is doing. Words that tell us what someone is doing are called doing verbs. Every sentence must have at least one verb.

For example: He **played** with the kitten. She **walked** to the shop.

**1** Read the story about the big game. Write the missing doing verbs.

a What did the Mighty Ogs do? They _____ out onto the field.

b What did the umpire do? He _____ the ball.

c What did big Toddy do? Big Toddy _____ the ball.

d What did tiny Tommy do? He _____ with the ball and

then he _____ the ball to Terri Og.

e What did Terri Og do? She _____ the ball and then _____ it.

f What did the ball do? The ball _____ near Timmy Og.

g What did Timmy Og do? Timmy _____ the ball up.

Timmy _____ and _____ around the Ug defenders.

Timmy _____ the ball through the goals.

h What did the Ug players do? The Ug players _____ .

i What does Coach Olly Og do? He _____ out his hair.

**2** Choose a doing verb from the box that would best complete these sentences.

a The Ogs _____ onto the football field.

b He _____ towards the goal post.

c They _____ striped jumpers.

d The coach _____ his own hair.

> pulled
> ran
> kicked
> wore

**TAKE THE CHALLENGE**

Circle five doing verbs that tell us what you can do in the playground at lunchtime.

run   chase   sit   stand   fly   skip   kick   swim   eat   write   drink   climb

grow   draw   catch   melt   play   sink   dig   explode   disappear   read

# A dark and stormy night

It was a dark and stormy night.

Two large, mean dragons and a small, timid dragon sheltered in a cave. The two large, mean dragons turned to the smaller dragon.

"Tell us a story or we'll toss you out!" they growled. Quaking with fright, the timid dragon began his story.

"It was a dark and stormy night," he whispered. "Two large, mean dragons and a small, timid dragon sheltered in a cave. The two large, mean dragons turned to the smaller dragon."

"Tell us a story or we'll toss you out!" they grumbled. Quaking with fright, the timid dragon began his story.

"It was a dark and stormy night," he whimpered. "Two large, mean dragons and a small, timid dragon sheltered in a cave. The two large, mean dragons turned to the smaller dragon."

"Tell us a story or we'll toss you out!" they shouted. Quaking with fright, the timid dragon began his story.

"It was a dark and stormy night," he sighed. "Two large, mean ..."

*Traditional*

Some verbs tell us the way someone is talking. These verbs are called saying verbs. We can get to know characters in stories better through the way they speak.

For example: *The dragons **growled**. "That's funny!" the children **giggled**.*

**1** Read 'A dark and stormy night'. Which three saying verbs tell us the way the small dragon spoke?

a  w _____

b  w _____

c  s _____

**2** Which three saying verbs tell us the way the two large dragons spoke to the small dragon?

a  g _____

b  g _____

c  s _____

**3** Use saying verbs from the box to complete these sentences.

> groaned     whispered     laughed     asked     screamed     ordered

a  "That's so funny," _____ Briana.

b  "Oh no! Not Maths again," _____ the children.

c  "Where do you live?" _____ Mr Bright.

d  "Look out! It's going to hit you!" _____ Tim.

e  "Ssh or she will hear us." _____ Erin.

f  "Please keep to the left," _____ the police officer.

**TAKE THE CHALLENGE**

On a piece of paper, write your own sentences using these saying verbs.

yelled          giggled          asked          shouted          begged

# The Ogs at school

Toddy Og believes in UFOs.

Danny Og imagines dragons in days of old.

Tammy Og hopes the swimming pool stays open late tonight.

Tilly Og enjoys her Ogomobile on weekends.

Ollie Og wonders why Ogs have to go to school.

BORING

Teddy Og decides on a Carrot Icy Blast for his after-school treat.

Mr B Og realises that none of the Ogs are paying attention.

Some verbs tell us about the way we think and feel.

These verbs are called thinking and feeling verbs.

For example: *I **think** fruit is good for you. We **love** playing outside.*

**1** Read 'The Ogs at school', then underline the thinking or feeling verbs in the sentences below.

a   Tilly Og enjoys her Ogomobile on weekends.

b   Ollie Og wonders why Ogs have to go to school.

c   Tammy Og hopes the swimming pool stays open late tonight.

d   Toddy Og believes in UFOs.

e   Teddy Og decides on a Carrot Icy Blast for his after-school treat.

**2** Write thinking or feeling verbs to complete the sentences below.

a   Danny Og _____ dragons in days of old.

b   Mr B Og _____ that none of the Ogs are paying attention.

**3** a   Circle the thinking or feeling verb in the following sentences.

Alice noticed a large, red toadstool growing nearby. She wondered why it was such an unusual colour.

b   Now, in the thought bubble, write what Alice was wondering.

**TAKE THE CHALLENGE**

Write your own sentences, using these thinking or feeling verbs.

wish          remember          know          need

_____

_____

_____

_____

# Billy Bud

Billy Bud washed his hair before he went to bed,
But Billy Bud used Green-Gro from his Daddy's shed.
Well foolish Billy has no hair upon his silly head,
For now he has a garden growing there instead.
Pretty little primroses growing in a row,
Daffodils and jonquils put on a lovely show.
Then there is a vegie patch to hoe, hoe, hoe,
And of course the grassy lawn which Billy needs to mow.

*AjW*

'Being' or 'having' words are called relating verbs.
The most common relating verbs are: *am, is, are, was, were, has, have, had*

**1** Read the poem about Billy Bud and then use relating verbs from the box to fill the gaps in the sentences.

> am    is    are    was    were    has    have    had

a   Billy _____ no hair upon his head.

b   There _____ a vegie patch over there.

c   Billy _____ naughty to go into Daddy's shed.

d   There _____ primroses growing in a row.

e   _____ you ever been foolish like Billy?

f   Daffodils and jonquils _____ flowers.

g   Daddy saw that Billy _____ a garden growing on his head.

h   "I _____ a foolish boy," said Billy.

**2** Use relating verbs from the box in question 1 to fill the gaps in Karli's 'School Garden Report'.

### SCHOOL GARDEN REPORT by Karli Tonetti

In our school we _____ a lovely garden. Part of the garden _____

filled with flowers and shrubs. Some of the flowers _____ fragrant. We also

_____ a large kitchen garden. I _____ in charge of the herb section.

This year our school _____ awarded a certificate for the Best Kitchen Garden.

We _____ all very proud of our garden.

**TAKE THE CHALLENGE**

Circle the relating verbs in these sentences.

a   'Ogs Ahoy!' is a funny story about the adventures of Toddy Og.

b   Bees have a very important role to play in pollinating plants.

c   Molly and Ravi are the fastest runners in Year 3.

# Cooky's diary

## Tuesday

**On Tuesday, Cooky prepared for her TV cooking show by writing down what she was going to do.**

I will need two eggs, some milk, some butter and two pieces of bread.

I will mix the eggs, milk and butter in a bowl.

I will pour the mixture into my frying pan and I will cook it slowly until the eggs are fluffy.

I will toast the bread.

When my eggs are ready, I will put them on the toast and serve them.

## Wednesday

**On Wednesday, it was time for Cooky's show. She explained to the viewers what she was doing as she prepared her meal.**

First, I am getting two eggs, some milk and some butter from the fridge. Now, I am cutting two pieces of bread ready for toasting.

I am mixing the eggs, milk and butter in a bowl.

I am pouring the mixture into my frying pan and I am cooking it slowly until the eggs are fluffy.

Now that my pieces of bread are toasted I am putting the eggs on them.

Yummm! They taste great.

## Thursday

**On Thursday, Cooky thought that she had better jot down in her diary what she had done on the show the night before. Here is what she wrote.**

First I took two eggs, some milk and some butter from the fridge.

Then I broke the eggs into a bowl and added the milk and butter. I mixed them up and then I poured them into my frying pan.

I cooked the mixture slowly.

When my bread was toasted I served up the eggs and ate the lot. My scrambled eggs were delicious.

Verbs can tell what happened then (in the past). For example: *Yesterday I **watched** the game.*
Verbs can tell what is happening now (in the present). For example: *I **am watching** the game.*
Verbs can tell what will happen later (in the future). For example: *Tomorrow I **will watch** the game.*

**1** Read 'Cooky's diary', then write whether the following sentences tell what has happened (past), what is happening (present) or what will happen (future).

a  I am getting my eggs out of the fridge. _____

b  I cooked the mixture slowly. _____

c  I took some milk from the fridge. _____

d  Now I am mixing the eggs, milk and butter. _____

e  When I have mixed the eggs, milk and butter I will pour them into a frying pan.

_____

f  I will need eggs, milk and butter. _____

**2** a  Write a sentence about something you did yesterday. Underline the verb(s).

Yesterday, I _____ .

b  Write a sentence about something that you are doing now. Underline the verb(s).

I am _____ .

c  Write a sentence about something you will do tomorrow. Underline the verb(s).

Tomorrow, _____ .

**3** Choose from these verbs/verb groups to write three sentences – one sentence about the past, one sentence about the present and one about the future.

| Past | Present | Future |
|------|---------|--------|
| played | are playing | will play |
| have written | am writing | will write |
| visited | is visiting | will visit |

_____

_____

_____

**TAKE THE CHALLENGE**

Make a prediction! On a piece of paper, write three sentences to say what you may be doing in a week's time, on this day next year and when you are an adult.

# I must remember!

Some verbs are helping verbs. They are always used with another verb. Sometimes they tell how sure we are about doing something. They are called modal verbs.

*will, can, shall, must* are modal verbs we use when we are sure: *I* **must** *go.*
*might, could, should, may* are modal verbs we use when we are not sure: *I* **might** *go.*

Modal verbs are helping verbs. They are always used with another verb.

**1** Read the comic strip on page 34. Write the missing modal verbs used as helping verbs in each sentence.

a "There's something I _____ remember," said Taddy Og.

b "I know there's something I _____ remember," said Taddy Og.

c "What was that thing I _____ forget?" wondered Taddy Og.

d "I _____ forget to plug the hole in my boat!" sighed Taddy Og.

**2** Rewrite each of these sentences, changing the modal verb underlined so the writer sounds really sure about doing something.

a I might go to the movies.

_____

b My friend Jack may come with us.

_____

c We could take more care when crossing busy roads.

_____

**TAKE THE CHALLENGE**

Choose modal verbs from the box and write them in the gaps to help show how sure the writer is about each of the verbs underlined.

a I _____ **watch** a movie tonight.

b Tess _____ **catch** with both hands.

c We _____ **hurry** or we _____ **miss** the bus.

d You _____ **brush** your teeth after every meal.

should
will
might
can

# The adventures of Adverb Man

The twins are in trouble!

Adverb Man flies quickly to the rescue.

The bad guys tremble fearfully.

Adverb Man powerfully lifts the evil monsters.

Adverb Man fights ferociously. THUD! BIFF POW!

Sigh! My hero who bravely came to my rescue.

Yay! A-Man!

The crowd cheers loudly for our hero.

Did he use his heat vision today?

Is it a bird flying swiftly?

Is it a plane soaring rapidly?

Adverbs add details about verbs.

Adverbs often answer the questions: How? When? Where?

Many adverbs end in **-ly** (*quickly, silently, happily, carefully*) but some don't (*yesterday, now, there, fast*).

For example:   *He walks **slowly**. (How does he walk? **slowly**)*

*She knew **immediately**. (When did she know? **immediately**)*

*They stopped **here**. (Where did they stop? **here**)*

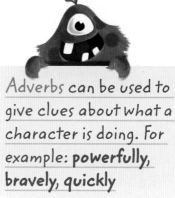

Adverbs can be used to give clues about what a character is doing. For example: **powerfully, bravely, quickly**

**1**  Use the comic strip on page 36 to write one adverb to answer each of these questions.

a   How does Adverb Man fly to the rescue? _____

b   How does Adverb Man lift the evil monsters? _____

c   How does Adverb Man fight? _____

d   How do the bad guys tremble? _____

**2**  Use adverbs from the comic strip that add details about the verbs underlined.

a   a bird <u>flying</u> _____

b   a plane <u>soaring</u> _____

c   a crowd <u>cheering</u> _____

d   a hero <u>rescuing</u> children _____

Adverbs can be added to verbs to make our opinion stronger when we are talking about a story or film.

For example: *I like Adverb Man. I **really** like Adverb Man.*

Adverbs can be added to adjectives to make our opinion stronger.

For example: *Adverb Man is fantastic! Adverb Man is **so** fantastic!*

Modal adverbs can be used to show how sure we are about something.

For example: *I would **probably** go to see the movie again. I would **definitely** go to see the movie again.*

**3**  Use the adverb *very* to write your opinion of Adverb Man.

_____

_____

_____

## TAKE THE CHALLENGE

Write adverbs to answer these questions.

a   How might a spider crawl? _____

b   How might an injured person stagger? _____

# The monkey and the crocodile

**Read the story about the monkey and the crocodile with your teacher.**

Once, a monkey lived in a great tree by a river. In the river were savage crocodiles.

One day the King Crocodile said to a smaller crocodile, "See that monkey in the treetop; I want to eat his heart. Get him for me."

The smaller crocodile thought about how he could catch the monkey. "I do not travel on the land and the monkey will not travel in the water. I will have to play a trick on him."

The crocodile swam until he was under the tree.

"Oh, Monkey!" he called. "There is some juicy ripe fruit on the island in the middle of the river. Why don't you go and get some?"

"Don't be silly, Crocodile," said the monkey. "I cannot swim."

"I will take you on my back," said the crocodile with a smile.

When the crocodile came up again the monkey sputtered, "Why are you trying to drown me?"

"I am going to kill you and give your heart to my king," said the crocodile.

"Why Crocodile, if I'd have known you wanted my heart, I would have brought it with me but I have left it in my treetop. If you want it, we could go back and fetch it."

The stupid crocodile agreed to take the monkey back to the tree to fetch his heart.

Of course, as soon as they had reached the shore, the monkey scampered up into the treetop. From the safety of his tree the monkey called down to the crocodile, "Nyahh! Nyahh! Stupid Crocodile! If you want my heart then you will have to climb my tree to get it!"

And with that the crocodile knew that he had been tricked by Monkey and both of them had learnt important lessons.

The greedy monkey wanted the fruit, so he jumped onto the back of the crocodile and off they went.

When the crocodile had reached deep water, he suddenly dived. The monkey was frightened. He did not like going under the water.

OXFORD UNIVERSITY PRESS

A phrase is a small group of words without a verb.
For example: *in the tree, on the land, under the bridge, over here!*
Phrases can add details about how, when or where.

**1** Use the phrases in the box to answer these questions about the story.

> to his king                    in a great tree
> in the middle of the river     on the land
> by a river                     on the island
> on the crocodile's back        under the water

a   Where did the monkey live? _____

b   Where was the great tree? _____

c   Where couldn't the crocodile travel? _____

d   Where was the juicy ripe fruit? _____

e   Where was the island? _____

f   How did Monkey travel across the water? _____

g   Where did the crocodile dive? _____

h   Where was Crocodile going to take Monkey's heart? _____

**2** Use phrases to answer these questions about your school.
For example:   *Where is your teacher?*
              *out the front, at her desk, at home sick, in the staffroom, etc.*

a   Where is the clock? _____

b   Where do you sit? _____

c   Where do you keep your pencils? _____

d   Where do you eat lunch? _____

**TAKE THE CHALLENGE**

Jokes and riddles are often answered with phrases.
Can you match these jokes and the phrases that are the answers?

Where did the King keep his armies?          **with a laser blade**
How does a robot alien shave?                **with their mountaineers**
How do mountains hear?                       **up his sleevies**

# It's Eid ul-Fitr!

Eid ul-Fitr (say *eed-ool-fit-r*) is a wonderful time. It is a time to celebrate.

Aisha's family are Muslim people.

Each year Aisha and her family observe Ramadan which lasts for 30 days. During Ramadan, Aisha can only eat and drink after sunset. She must fast during daylight hours.

The festival of Eid ul-Fitr follows Ramadan. Muslim people happily visit each other. They generously give money to help poor people. During the festival, they dress in their best clothes.

*Meethai*

The part of Eid ul-Fitr that Aisha enjoys enthusiastically is the delicious food that is served. For three days Aisha gets to eat yummy treats like these:

- fruit chaat, which is a spiced fruit salad

- meethai, which is a selection of sweet meats, and

- Aisha's favourite, sheer khurma, which is a pudding cooked in sweet milk and flavoured with dates.

*Sheer khurma*

All these tantalising treats are gobbled up hungrily by Aisha, her brothers and sisters and cousins.

**1** Underline the verbs in each of these sentences.

   **a** Aisha celebrates Eid ul-Fitr after Ramadan.

   **b** During Eid ul-Fitr people happily visit each other.

   **c** Aisha hopes there are delicious treats on the table.

   **d** "It's Eid ul-Fitr!" shouted the children excitedly.

**2** Use adverbs from the box to fill the gaps in these sentences.

> Be careful where you place a phrase in a sentence. Can you see why these sentences might confuse a reader? She gave a box to the teacher that was made of metal. The dog gnawed the bone with sharp teeth.

> happily    hungrily    generously    tomorrow

   **a** The children gobbled up the treats _____ .

   **b** Ramadan will end _____ and Eid ul-Fitr will begin.

   **c** We visit each other _____ .

   **d** Aisha's family _____ donate money to help poor people.

**3** Underline the phrases in these sentences.

   **a** Wonderful treats were set upon the table.

   **b** Aisha must not eat or drink during daylight hours.

   **c** Sheer khurma is a pudding cooked in sweet milk.

## TAKE THE CHALLENGE

Write modal verbs from the box in these sentences.

   **a** Muslims _____ fast during Ramadan.

   **b** Aisha and her family _____ celebrate Eid ul-Fitr every year.

   **c** The children are excited that they _____ see wonderful treats on the table.

> might
> should
> will

# TOPIC 2: TEST YOUR GRAMMAR!

## Verbs, adverbs and phrases

**1** Shade the bubble below the doing verb in this sentence.

*Maggie walked to the shops before breakfast.*

○      ○      ○          ○

**2** Shade the bubble next to the word that is a doing verb.

○ she          ○ drank          ○ glass          ○ milk

**3** Shade the bubble next to the saying verb.

○ thought          ○ caught          ○ cried          ○ could

**4** Shade the bubble next to the saying verb that would best complete this sentence.

*"That's the funniest joke I've heard all day,"* ⬭ *Ruby.*

○ shouted          ○ asked          ○ screamed          ○ chuckled

**5** Shade the bubble next to the thinking or feeling verb.

○ played          ○ does          ○ wished          ○ laughed

**6** Shade the bubble below the thinking or feeling verb in this sentence.

*We like the colour of our new car.*

○      ○      ○ ○

**7** Shade the bubble below the thinking or feeling verb in this sentence.

*Tom remembered that his homework was due on Friday.*

○      ○      ○          ○

**8** Shade the bubble below the verb in this sentence.

*The train arrived at the railway station.*

    ○    ○       ○      ○

**9** Shade the bubble below the relating verb in this sentence.

*My book has a lot of exciting chapters.*

  ○  ○  ○      ○

**10** Shade the bubble next to the sentence that describes something that happened in the past.

○ We rode our horses along Simpson's Lane.

○ We will ride our horses along Simpson's Lane.

○ We are riding our horses along Simpson's Lane.

○ We are going to ride our horses along Simpson's Lane.

**11** Shade the bubble next to the words that form the verb in this sentence.

*We might catch an early train to the city.*

○ We might    ○ might catch    ○ an early    ○ to the city

**12** Shade the bubble next to the adverb.

○ lifts    ○ beautiful    ○ hero    ○ bravely

**13** Shade the bubble next to the phrase.

○ in the tree    ○ am running    ○ will play    ○ are smiling

## HOW AM I DOING?

Colour the boxes if you understand.

Verb can be doing, saying, thinking or feeling words. ☐

Some verbs are 'being' or 'having' words. ☐

Verbs can tell us when things happen. ☐

Adverbs tell us more about verbs. ☐

Phrases are small groups of words without a verb. ☐

## UNIT 3.1 Text cohesion – antonyms

# THE GREAT ANTO NYM

Anto Nym is one of the famous Nym Brothers. He is a circus acrobat.

Today he is going to walk the tightrope.

Anto Nym comes inside the circus tent and starts his act by saying hello.

He begins to climb up a high ladder.

When he is at the top, the bright lights go dim. A spotlight shines on Anto. He takes his first step forwards. Everybody is quiet. Nobody makes a sound.

SLIP!

EEK!

GASP!

When Anto Nym reaches the middle, he slips. The crowd cries in horror. Anto is in great danger, for there is no net. He grabs the rope and swings back up onto his feet.

He bows comically to the crowd. The crowd laughs and gives him loud applause.

When Anto takes his last step and reaches the safety of the other side, there is more clapping and cheering. He climbs down the ladder.

Anto finishes his act by waving goodbye to the crowd. He walks backwards and goes outside where his brothers, Syno and Hommy, are waiting to perform.

Some words have opposites. These are called antonyms.

For example: *tall* and *short*, *back* and *front*, *day* and *night*, *shut* and *open*

**1** Read the story about Anto Nym and find the words that are antonyms for these words.

a  up _____

b  first _____

c  hello _____

d  inside _____

e  starts _____

f  bright _____

g  cries _____

h  quiet _____

i  forwards _____

j  comes _____

k  danger _____

l  everybody _____

**2** Write words from the box that are antonyms of these words.

straight   thin   defend   sunset   weak   old
love   stale   buy   steep

a  thick _____

b  sell _____

c  strong _____

d  flat _____

e  young _____

f  attack _____

g  fresh _____

h  hate _____

i  bent _____

j  sunrise _____

Sometimes we can add a prefix to the start of a word to make an antonym (opposite).

For example: *un* + *happy* = *unhappy* (*happy* and *unhappy* are opposites)

*dis* + *like* = *dislike* (*like* and *dislike* are opposites)

**3** Add the prefixes *un* or *dis* to these words to make antonyms.

a  _____appear

b  _____real

c  _____kind

d  _____do

e  _____honest

f  _____friendly

g  _____fair

h  _____lock

i  _____agree

j  _____dress

k  _____tie

l  _____obey

**TAKE THE CHALLENGE**

Add a prefix to these words to make them antonyms.

a  _____possible

b  _____safe

c  _____connect

d  _____direct

e  _____twist

f  _____visible

# Syno Nym the acrobat

Syno Nym the acrobat arrives. The crowd claps.

and glides, wobbles, slides, shakes and skims until … he disappears.

Syno stretches and bends. The crowd waits. Syno limbers up and flexes. The Great Syno is ready.

Amazing!

The crowd cheers. They want more, but…

More!

…Syno is busy yelling and screaming at Blip the Clown who has left his skateboard in the wrong place again!

OXFORD UNIVERSITY PRESS

Some words have the same or nearly the same meaning as other words. These words are called synonyms. For example: In the story, *jumps* could be replaced with *leaps* or *springs*.

*Runs* could be replaced with *races* or *hurries*.

**1** Find words in the story about Syno Nym that are synonyms for these words.

a twirls _____

b vanishes _____

c enters _____

d awaits _____

e yelling _____

f incorrect _____

g audience _____

h sprints _____

i expands _____

j prepared _____

**2** Draw lines to match the words in Box A with their synonyms in Box B.

claps   slides   flexes   flies   more   jumps   **A**

soars   bends   applauds   extra   glides   vaults   **B**

Words that have the same or nearly the same meaning are called synonyms.

**3** Find words in the word find that are synonyms for the words in the box.

| X | S | Z | H | J | Q | G | U |
|---|---|---|---|---|---|---|---|
| Q | H | B | V | U | N | V | N |
| B | I | G | R | I | R | W | H |
| E | P | K | R | O | V | T | A |
| N | E | A | R | X | O | Y | P |
| T | L | V | Z | K | T | M | P |
| B | A | N | D | I | T | N | Y |
| C | O | R | R | E | C | T | X |

boat
brush
circle
close
crooked
large
outlaw
injure
right
sad

**TAKE THE CHALLENGE**

Use a dictionary to help you find synonyms for these words. Write your answers on a separate piece of paper.

fear   create   mimic   bulky   hideous

# It's all about spiders!

Spiders and their close relatives, the scorpions, are called *arachnids*. To some people, spiders can be terrifying creatures. This fear of spiders is called *arachnophobia* (say **uh-rack-nuh-foh-bee-uh**). Let's look at some spiders to see if they deserve their reputation.

Huntsman spiders, although big and hairy, are generally harmless. They are actually more frightened of you than you need to be of them. They will only bite if threatened, preferring to run away. Huntsman spiders are good pest controllers to have around the house as they eat flies, mosquitoes and other nuisance pests.

Not so harmless are the male Sydney funnel-web spider and the female redback spider. Both of these spiders are highly venomous and they are the only Australian spiders known to have caused deaths.

There is no scientific evidence to support the myth that the venom of the daddy-long-legs spider is the most toxic of all spiders. The daddy-long-legs spider's fangs are tiny and are not capable of penetrating human skin.

So, as long as we take sensible precautions like shaking out footwear and clothing before putting it on, there really is no need to fear our eight-legged friends.

OXFORD UNIVERSITY PRESS

Writers use paragraphs to organise information. Paragraphs usually start with a topic sentence to introduce the main point being made in the paragraph. The sentences that follow usually provide us with further details about the topic sentence.

**1** Read the report about spiders. There are five paragraphs. Write first, second, third, fourth or last to say which paragraphs match these descriptions.

a   I am a paragraph about a spider myth. _____

b   I am a paragraph about venomous spiders in Australia. _____

c   I am a paragraph about huntsman spiders. _____

d   I am the concluding paragraph. _____

e   I am the introductory paragraph that classifies spiders. _____

**2** Copy the topic sentence from the introductory paragraph that classifies spiders.

_____

_____

_____

**3** Write your own paragraph in which the main idea is about sharks or snakes and the starting topic is about the fear of these creatures.

_____

_____

_____

_____

_____

**TAKE THE CHALLENGE**

Information reports such as this one about spiders often include some technical language or scientific terms. Read the report again and write any words you think are scientific words that could be used about spiders.

_____

_____

# Rain

It's good to lie in bed at night
And hear the sweeping rain
Go patter patter on the roof
And knock against the pane

It croaks and gurgles down the spout,
And swishes through the leaves,
And makes the curly creeper drip
That twines about the eaves.

All snug and warm in blankets soft
I hear a windy song
Like curlews in the lonely bush
That wail the whole night long.

**L. H. Allen**

OXFORD UNIVERSITY PRESS

Poets often use rhythm, alliteration and onomatopoeia to make their poems entertaining and easy to read.

Rhythm is the regular beat that makes the poem easy to read.

Alliteration is a group of words that begin with the same letter or sound. For example: *six silly sausages*

Onomatopoeia (say *on-oh-mat-uh-pee-uh*) is when words sound like the thing they are describing. For example: *Shush! Sizzle! Crack!*

**1** Read 'Rain'. The writer has used onomatopoeia to show the reader the sounds he thinks rain makes. On the line below, write the onomatopoeic words the poet has used to describe rain.

_____

**2** Circle the examples of onomatopoeia used in these sentences.

a   All night long the leaking tap went drip, drip drip.

b   "Achoo!" sneezed Bert, who had caught a cold.

c   When Tim poured milk onto his cereal it crackled and crunched.

d   All we could see was the flutter of butterfly wings.

**3** Tick the sentence below that shows the best example of alliteration.

a   Patter patter on the roof.

b   Patter patter on the pane.

c   Snug and warm in blankets soft.

**4** Use onomatopoeia and the rhythm and rhyme of this poem to complete the final line in your own words.

Here comes trotting Dobbin

with old Harry up on top,

Here he comes a'cantering

_____

**TAKE THE CHALLENGE**

The poem describes a wailing curlew. What do you think a curlew might be?

_____

# Jiemba

Hi, my name is Jiemba.

I live in Yirrkala which is in Arnhem Land in the Northern Territory of Australia.

Aboriginal people have lived in Yirrkala for a very long time.

Where I live is tropical which means it is warm all year round. That means that I can spend lots of time outside.

Living in a tropical place also means that, during the wet season, there might be cyclones. My school has been specially built to withstand a cyclone.

School where I live is not compulsory but I go anyway. Many of the lessons at my school are taught outside. We learn practical things like how to fish and hunt.

I like the bush and when I grow up I want to be a ranger like my dad. That way, I can teach other people about the bush.

**1** Find words in the text on page 52 that are antonyms for these words.

a cool _____

b dry _____

c short _____

d inside _____

**2** Draw lines from the words in Box A to their synonyms in Box B.

**A**
live
many
like
tropical
teach

**B**
instruct
hot
reside
enjoy
lots

**3** Use words from the box to complete these lines of alliteration.

fish   butter   rugged   saucepan

a Seven savoury sausages sizzling in a _____ .

b Forty funny flying _____ with five fins each.

c Bobbi Barker's baking bread to spread a bit of _____ on.

d Round and round the _____ rock the ragged rascal ran.

**TAKE THE CHALLENGE**

Can you add onomatopoeic words of your own to these pictures?

# TOPIC 3: TEST YOUR GRAMMAR!

## Text cohesion and language devices

**1** Shade the bubble next to the antonym (opposite) of the word **under**.
- ◯ inside
- ◯ over
- ◯ up
- ◯ below

**2** Shade the bubble next to the antonym (opposite) of the word **wide**.
- ◯ broad
- ◯ heavy
- ◯ narrow
- ◯ thick

**3** Shade the bubble next to the antonym (opposite) of the word **beautiful**.
- ◯ ugly
- ◯ nice
- ◯ attractive
- ◯ handsome

**4** Shade the bubble next to the antonym of the word **visible**.
- ◯ unvisible
- ◯ imvisible
- ◯ invisible
- ◯ disvisible

**5** Shade the bubble next to the prefix that can be added to **honest** to make it an opposite.
- ◯ un
- ◯ mis
- ◯ in
- ◯ dis

**6** Shade the bubble next to the prefix that can be added to **behave** to make it an opposite.
- ◯ un
- ◯ mis
- ◯ in
- ◯ dis

**7** Shade the bubble next to the synonym for **messy**.
- ◯ neat
- ◯ untidy
- ◯ lovely
- ◯ new

**8** Shade the bubble next to the synonym for **old**.
- ◯ new
- ◯ clear
- ◯ modern
- ◯ ancient

OXFORD UNIVERSITY PRESS

**9** Shade the bubble next to the synonym for **cries**.

○ sweeps      ○ weeps      ○ sweets      ○ peeps

**10** Read this paragraph.

*Syno Nym, the acrobat, entered the arena. The crowd clapped and Syno began his act.*

*He stretched and bent then ran, jumped and soared. He landed cleanly on his feet and*

*bowed to the audience.*

Now shade the bubble next to the topic sentence from the above paragraph.

○ Syno Nym, the acrobat, entered the arena.
○ The crowd clapped and Syno began his act.
○ He stretched and bent, then ran, jumped and soared.
○ He landed cleanly on his feet and bowed to the audience.

**11** Shade the bubble next to the example of onomatopoeia.

○ clear      ○ water      ○ splash      ○ surf

**12** Shade the bubble next to the example of alliteration.

○ pop! bang! crash!    ○ on the road      ○ one, two, three      ○ five fine fellows

**HOW AM I DOING?**

Colour the boxes if you understand.

Antonyms are opposites. ☐

Synonyms are words that mean the same or nearly the same. ☐

Paragraphs are used to organise information. ☐

A topic sentence introduces the main point of a paragraph. ☐

Rhythm, alliteration and onomatopoeia can be used to make text, especially poetry, more entertaining. ☐

# WHERE'S DAD?

OXFORD UNIVERSITY PRESS

A simple sentence is a group of words that make sense.

On their own, the following groups do not make sense:

*is sitting    the bird    on the branch*

If we reorder the groups and put them together, they make sense.

*The bird is sitting on the branch.* OR *On the branch the bird is sitting.*

OR *Sitting on the branch is the bird.*

All of these groups of words make sense. They are simple sentences.

A simple sentence has only one verb or verb group. For example:
**The bird is sitting on the branch.**

**1** Add your own words to make simple sentences.

a   On the weekend _____ .

b   The dog ran out of _____ .

c   _____ into the swimming pool.

**2** Join the sentence parts from each box so that you make four simple sentences about the picture opposite.

**Who or what?**

| Dad Galoot ... | The kookaburra ... | Zip ... | |
| Zac ... | Zig and Zed ... | Zeke ... | Mum Galoot ... |

**Is doing what?**

| ... is resting ... | ... are fighting ... |
| ... is sleeping ... | ... is calling ... |
| ... is laughing ... | ... is perched ... |
| ... is looking ... | ... is aiming ... |
| ... is playing ... | ... is running ... |

**When? Where? How? Why?**

| ... under the gum tree. | ... with Zeke. |
| ... around the tree. | ... at Zip. |
| ... for Dad Galoot. | ... on a branch. |
| ... at a can. | ... from the porch. |
| ... with each other. | ... after breakfast. |

_____

_____

_____

_____

**TAKE THE CHALLENGE**

On a piece of paper, unjumble these words to write one sentence.

on    farm    the    live    Galoots    The    a    in    country

# Zoot Galoot at the Olympics

Zoot Galoot is at the Olympic Games. He has entered many events.

Zoot jumps very high. No one cheers.

Zoot scores all the goals. There is no cheering.

Zoot throws the shot-put. He sets a new record.

Zoot wins the race. He is the only runner.

Perhaps Zoot should have gone INSIDE the Olympic Stadium for his events.

OXFORD UNIVERSITY PRESS

Coordinating conjunctions (*and, but, so* and *or*) can be used to join simple sentences together to form longer, compound sentences.

For example: *The goblin was small **and** he was very strong.*

*Akmed tried hard **but** he lost the game.*

*The plant died **so** we put it into the compost bin.*

Compound sentences have two verbs or verb groups. For example: *The goblin was small, but he was strong.*

**1** Read the story about Zoot Galoot, then join these simple sentences by using a coordinating conjunction (*and, but, or, so*).

a  Zoot jumps very high. No one cheers.

_____

b  Zoot is the only runner. He wins the race.

_____

c  Zoot throws the shot-put. He sets a new record.

_____

d  Zoot scores lots of goals. There is no cheering.

_____

**2** Rewrite these sentences as compound sentences by joining them with *and, but, or* or *so.*

a  It was raining. We couldn't go outside.

_____

b  We watered the seedlings often. They grew into pretty flowers.

_____

c  I would write it down. I don't have a pencil.

_____

**3** Circle the coordinating conjunctions in question 2 above.

## TAKE THE CHALLENGE

Complete these sentences in your own words.

a  I ran out of the room **and** _____.

b  _____ **but** I didn't go.

c  We arrived at the zoo early **so** _____.

# THE OGS' BIRTHDAY PARTY

OXFORD UNIVERSITY PRESS

We can change short sentences into longer, more interesting sentences by:
• adding phrases
• using conjunctions
• adding adjectives and adverbs.
For example: *Og O is blowing out candles.* could become …
*Og O is on the table blowing out three candles on a huge birthday cake.*

**1** Use the picture on page 60 to help you make longer, more interesting sentences below.

a Og G has a frying pan.

_____

b Og D is climbing a ladder.

_____

c Og U is in a car.

_____

d Og T has a balloon.

_____

e There is a paddle pool.

_____

**2** Add a phrase to write a longer, more interesting sentence below.

The Ogs are having a birthday party.

_____

_____

_____

## TAKE THE CHALLENGE

On a piece of paper, write three of your own longer, more interesting sentences about the picture – one using a phrase (or phrases), one using a coordinating conjunction (**and**, **but**, **or**, **so**) and one using at least one adjective and one adverb.
For example: *Og W is happily running into the busy room.*

# Why the honeybee stings

## A tale from Ancient Greece

The honeybee was unhappy. People were stealing her honey. The honeybee thought that all of the honey should be hers. She did not want to share any honey.

The honeybee went to Zeus, who was the chief god. She asked Zeus to give her the power to sting anyone who came near her hive. Zeus granted the honeybee's wish.

However, he was angry that the honeybee would be so mean. Zeus decided to teach her a lesson. He cast a spell that made the honeybee lose her sting when she used it on anyone.

Of course, today we know that honeybees do not only lose their stings when they use them. They also lose their lives.

OXFORD UNIVERSITY PRESS

Every simple sentence has a **subject** telling who or what the sentence is about. Every simple sentence also has a **verb**. The subject and verb must agree. For example:

✓ *The honeybee is in the hive.*      ✗ *The honeybee are in the hive.*

The second sentence is incorrect. It should be: *The honeybees are in the hive.*

**1** Read the story on page 62. Write a **subject** from the box to agree with the bolded verbs in these sentences.

> A simple sentence has one main idea or main clause. It always has a subject and a verb or verb group.

a _____ **was** unhappy.

b _____ **were stealing** honey.

c _____ **would not share** her honey.

d _____ **grants** the honeybee's wish.

e _____ **have** striped bodies.

f _____ **was** angry with the honeybee.

g _____ **was** very mean.

h _____ **know** all about honeybees now.

i _____ **have** a sting on their tail.

> Honeybees
>
> The honeybee
>
> Zeus
>
> We
>
> People

**2** Circle the **verb that agrees** correctly with the subject in each of the sentences below.

a The monster **is / are** scary.

b Humpty Dumpty **was / were** on the wall.

c The honeybee **sting / stings**.

d Dogs **bark / barks**.

e I **like / likes** fish.

f We **has / have** a new teacher.

g The ship **is / are** at the port.

h They **is / are** upset.

**3** Underline the **subjects** in these sentences.

a Tractors pull heavy logs.

b Dad made a billycart for the children.

c Giraffes have long necks.

d The ship sank quickly.

## TAKE THE CHALLENGE

Add your own **subjects** to finish these sentences.

a _____ was sitting at the bus stop waiting patiently.

b _____ barked when the stranger came into the garden.

# Common sense

## (A story from Africa)

Anansi the spider thought of a good idea. He would gather up all the common sense in the world. That would make Anansi very powerful and all the animals would need to come to him for advice.

Anansi went about collecting common sense. He put all of it into an empty gourd (a large fruit shell). Anansi decided to hide his gourd at the top of a very tall tree. He tied one end of a rope around the neck of the gourd. He tied the other end around his neck so the huge gourd hung in front of him.

Anansi tried to climb the tree but the gourd was in his way. He could not stretch his arms and legs around the tree's trunk.

Anansi heard some laughter. He looked around and saw Monkey.

"You are a silly fellow," said Monkey. "If you had any common sense you would hang that gourd on your back so you can climb the tree."

Anansi was furious because he realised that Monkey still had some common sense. He smashed the gourd against the tree and common sense scattered everywhere. It was carried all around the world by the wind. That is why today everybody has a little common sense.

1 Complete these simple sentences from the story on page 64.

a Anansi went about collecting _____ .

b _____ of a good idea.

c _____ some laughter.

2 Circle the coordinating conjunctions in these sentences from the story of Anansi.

Do you remember? Coordinating conjunctions can be used to join simple sentences together to make more interesting, longer sentences.

a He smashed the gourd against the tree and common sense scattered everywhere.

b Anansi tried to climb the tree but the gourd was in his way.

c He tied the other end around his neck so the huge gourd hung in front of him.

3 Circle the verb that agrees correctly with the subject in each of the sentences below.

a Common sense **was** / **were** scattered everywhere.

b The animals **is** / **are** coming to Anansi for advice.

c That is why today everybody **have** / **has** a little common sense.

**TAKE THE CHALLENGE**

Can you improve these sentences by joining them with one of these coordinating conjunctions?

and     but     so

a Anansi heard some laughter. He looked around.

_____

b Anansi stretched out his legs. They would not fit around the tree's trunk.

_____

# TOPIC 4: TEST YOUR GRAMMAR!

## Sentences

**1** Shade the bubble next to the simple sentence.

○ near the house
○ at sunset
○ We climbed the hill.
○ The weary walkers crossed the stream so they could reach the camp.

**2** Shade the bubble next to the group of words that could be added to the following sentence beginning to form a simple sentence.

*The girl* ⌈_____⌉

○ shut the window.　○ on the bridge　○ happy　○ quickly

**3** Shade the bubble next to the group of words that could be added to the following sentence ending to form a simple sentence.

⌈_____⌉ *at the clown.*

○ on fire　○ The circus　○ We laughed　○ was funny

**4** Shade the bubble next to the verb that completes this sentence.

*The children* ⌈_____⌉ *playing in the park.*

○ is　○ am　○ are　○ was

**5** Shade the bubble next to the verb that completes this sentence.

*Kangaroos* ⌈_____⌉ *in Australia.*

○ live　○ lived　○ lives　○ living

**6** Shade the bubble next to the verb that completes this sentence.

*We* ⌈_____⌉ *expecting the tram to arrive at 9 o'clock.*

○ is　○ were　○ was　○ am

OXFORD UNIVERSITY PRESS

**7** Shade the bubble next to the coordinating conjunction that best completes this sentence.

*The cat was tired* ( _____ ) *it curled up and went to sleep.*

○ and       ○ but       ○ so       ○ or

**8** Shade the bubble next to the coordinating conjunction that best completes this sentence.

*I made a cheese sandwich* ( _____ ) *I ate it for my lunch.*

○ and       ○ but       ○ so       ○ or

**9** Shade the bubble next to the coordinating conjunction that best completes this sentence.

*My Grandpa is very old* ( _____ ) *he is still fit and strong.*

○ and       ○ but       ○ so       ○ or

**10** Shade the bubble next to the sentence that is **not** a simple sentence.

○ Ducks like bread.
○ Skye is tall and she has dark hair.
○ The dog tried to steal the meat.
○ The sharp-eyed eagle soared majestically into the sky.

**11** Rewrite this simple sentence as a longer, more interesting sentence.
*Frogs croak.*

_____

## HOW AM I DOING?

Colour the boxes if you understand.

Sentences must make sense.  ☐

A simple sentence has one main idea or main clause and one verb or verb group.  ☐

The subject and the verb of a sentence must agree.  ☐

A compound sentence has two verbs or verb groups.  ☐

Coordinating conjunctions can be used to join simple sentences to make longer, more interesting sentences.  ☐

## UNIT 5.1   Capital letters

# Zoot Galoot - space ace!

Zoot Galoot, ace space pilot, relaxes in his comfy chair and flips a control button.

A Gorgon spacefighter from the Medusa Galaxy is heading straight at Zoot. He dives for cover.

Suddenly, a terrifying monster appears. It moves towards Zoot. The space ace covers his eyes.

A train appears from nowhere and charges at Zoot. He hides behind his comfy chair.

A great ball of fire hurtles towards Zoot. It is a comet. In a few seconds, Zoot will be smashed into a million pieces. There is nowhere left for Zoot to hide.

We'll be back after this short ad break.

So Zoot switches off the TV and goes outside to play.

The comet comes **closer,**

**closer,**

**closer...**

OXFORD UNIVERSITY PRESS

Capital letters are used at the beginning of sentences.
For example: *The spaceship crashed in the paddock.*

Use capital letters: at the beginning of a sentence, for proper nouns, for the word I.

**1** Read the story, then write the following sentences using the correct punctuation.

a   he is hiding behind his chair.

_____

b   a spacefighter is heading straight at him.

_____

c   in a few seconds, Zoot will be smashed into a million pieces.

_____

d   the fireball moves towards Zoot.

_____

Capital letters are used for special names (proper nouns) of people, places and things.

**2** Write these proper nouns using the correct punctuation.

a   zoot galoot _____      b   roald dahl _____

c   new south wales _____      d   sunday _____

e   hume freeway _____      f   january _____

**3** Rewrite the following sentences using the correct punctuation.

a   in the hall, i saw mr cheng's coat and new umbrella.

_____

b   ben, ari and i travelled together to sydney.

_____

c   when i saw elvis rasheed in knight street, i called out to him and waved.

_____

_____

The word *I* is always written with a capital letter.

**TAKE THE CHALLENGE**

On a piece of paper, use the correct punctuation to write the names of:

• three members of your family

• a good name for an alien spaceship

• the name of a book you have enjoyed reading

• five days of the week.

# How the Sun was made

LONG AGO the world was in darkness.

The animals and the birds lived by the light of the moon and stars. They knew only night.

In this time, Emu and Brolga began to quarrel over their eggs. Emu thought her egg was the most beautiful egg in the world. Brolga argued that her egg was far more beautiful than Emu's. They screeched and squawked at each other.

Brolga rushed at Emu's nest. She grabbed Emu's egg and tossed it high into the sky. In the sky, the egg struck a pile of wood that had been gathered by the Cloud Man. The wood burst into flames. The flames flooded the world with the soft, warm light of the first dawn. The flowers lifted their heads and opened their petals. The birds chirped and carolled. All of the animals stretched and looked up to welcome the dawn.

As the fire burned longer, the day became warmer and brighter. Later in the day, the fire began to burn low. The world became dull again. The Cloud Man thought the fire would be a good thing to have every day.

Now each night the Cloud Man gathers firewood. He builds up the fire so that the next day may be bright and warm for all of the world's creatures.

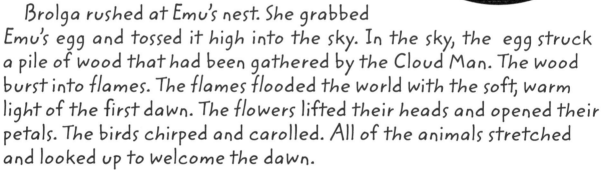

OXFORD UNIVERSITY PRESS

Statements are sentences that state facts, give opinions or tell information of some sort.
A statement always begins with a capital letter and ends with a full stop.
For example: *The animals, birds and plants knew only night.*

**1** Unjumble these words to write statements from the story.

a   the world Long ago in darkness. was

_____

b   nest. Brolga Emu's rushed at

_____

c   screeched and squawked They at each other.

_____

d   into flames. The wood burst

_____

**2** Write statements of your own using these beginnings.

a   On Tuesday afternoon _____.

b   Snakes are _____.

c   In the park beside the tree _____.

**3** Rewrite these statements, adding capital letters and full stops where they belong.

a   brolga rushed at emu's nest

_____

b   the flames flooded the world

_____

**4** Write statements of your own using these endings.

a   _____ my next birthday.

b   _____ in the forest.

**TAKE THE CHALLENGE**

On a piece of paper, write five statements that tell us something about you. Make sure that not all of your statements begin with **I** and that your statements are complete sentences.

# Don't ask me!

Uncle Rob, why is the sky so blue?

Don't ask me now, for I've work here to do.

Mum, why is the water in my bath so wet?

Don't ask me that, for I've shopping to get.

Sister Sue, why does the Sun chase after the Moon?

I'll answer that question on the thirty-first of June.

Tell me Dad, why does time fly when we're having fun?

Now, too many questions are not good for you, Son.

Why is that so, Dad? Won't you say more?

Save up your questions. What do you think school is for?

OXFORD UNIVERSITY PRESS

When we want an answer to something, we ask a question. A question ends with a question mark (**?**).
Some words that can ask questions are: *How? What? Where? When? Why?*

**1** Tick the sentences below that ask questions.

a Why is the sky so blue? ☐  b I've shopping to get. ☐

c When does time fly? ☐  d What do you think school is for? ☐

e Save up your questions, son. ☐  f Come here, son! ☐

g Is the Sun chasing the Moon? ☐  h Are you going to answer my questions? ☐

**2** Write questions that you think might have been asked to get the following answers.

a _____? My name is Marie.

b _____? I am nine years old.

c _____? My new jumper is red.

d _____? It is nearly three o'clock.

e _____? He told us to put our books away.

f _____?

On Saturday, I am going shopping for a birthday present.

g _____?

If the ball goes through the ring, your team scores two points.

**3** Write your own question in the speech bubble of this cartoon.

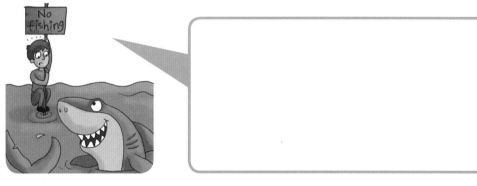

Questioning words are often used at the beginning of questions.
For example: **What** ? **How** ?
How many questioning words can you write?

# Pardon me!

All aboard!

Look out!

Kick it to me!

Go team!

Oh, my goodness! Midnight already!

Help! The giant's after me!

Open wide!

Boo!

Great work!

Troops! Advance!

Some sentences can be very short.

Some short sentences are called exclamations.

We use an exclamation when something is said suddenly, loudly and with feeling (fright, anger or pleasure).

An exclamation begins with a capital letter and ends with an exclamation mark (!).

For example: *Get out now!  Don't do that!*

**1** On the page opposite you can see ten exclamations and ten characters.

Write the best exclamation for each character in the spaces below.

a  " _____ " yelled the builder.

b  " _____ " cheered the sports fan.

c  " _____ " called the railway announcer.

d  " _____ " said the monster.

e  " _____ " called the football player.

f  " _____ " said the teacher.

g  " _____ " ordered the general.

h  " _____ " said the dentist.

i  " _____ " cried Jack.

j  " _____ " shrieked Cinderella.

**2** Write an exclamation for the cartoon below. Don't forget your exclamation mark!

## TAKE THE CHALLENGE

Write an exclamation that you might make:

• on your birthday. _____

• when your team scores the winning goal. _____

• when you are warning someone. _____

# What's in Nonny Og's shopping bag?

a long, thin, healthy loaf of bread

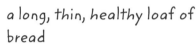

a packet of chewy, juicy Fruit Joobs

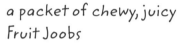

a bunch of large, ripe, yellow bananas, oranges, pears, grapes and apples

hard, holey cheese

potatoes, carrots, an eggplant, celery and a huge, round pumpkin

soft, squishy cheese

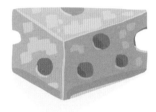

half a dozen delicious, farm-fresh, free-range eggs

and a large, gaping hole

OXFORD UNIVERSITY PRESS

Commas can be used to separate nouns in a list. For example: *horses, cows, ducks, pigs and sheep*
Commas can be used to separate adjectives in a list. For example: *the fast, new, red car*

**1** Read 'What's in Nonny Og's shopping bag?' and then add commas where you think they belong in these sentences.

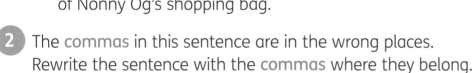

a Nonny Og bought apples oranges pears and grapes at the OgMart.

b There was a large gaping hole in the bottom of her shopping bag.

c The long thin loaf of bread was sticking out of the bag.

d The potatoes carrots eggplant and celery fell out of Nonny Og's shopping bag.

*Don't use a comma at the end of a list if the word and has been used. Don't use a comma to separate an adjective immediately before a noun.*

**2** The commas in this sentence are in the wrong places.
Rewrite the sentence with the commas where they belong.

*Nonny bought some soft squishy, cheese and some potatoes carrots, and pumpkin.*

_____

_____

_____

**TAKE THE CHALLENGE**

On a piece of paper, write three sentences listing your four favourite colours, six animals you might see at the zoo and five sports or games you like to watch or play. Don't forget to use commas to separate the things in your lists. Use these beginnings for your sentences.

My favourite colours are …

At the zoo I might see …

I like to watch or play …

# My puppy

It's funny
my puppy
knows just how I feel.
When I'm happy
he's yappy
and squirms like an eel.

When I'm grumpy
he's slumpy
and stays at my heel.
It's funny
my puppy
knows such a great
deal.

**Aileen Fisher**

# Mitch and Titch

Mitch went into a warm café
to escape the biting blizzard
and sitting upon his shoulder
there appeared to be a lizard.
"I think I'll have a tea," said Mitch
and, with a nod to the reptile, said,
"Titch here will have an orange juice
then I'll take him home to bed".
The waiter scratched her head and asked,
"Why do you call him Titch?"
"Now isn't that plainly obvious?
Cause he's my newt!" said Mitch.

*AjW*

Some words can be made shorter by leaving out letters.

When we are speaking informally with family or friends, words are often shortened by taking out letters. These shortened words are called contractions. We replace the letters with a mark like this '. This mark is called an apostrophe.

For example: *I'm = I am*   *we'll = we will*   *she'd = she would* or *she had*   *can't = can not*

**1** Write the contractions from the poems next to their partners below.

> it's       he's       I'll       I'm       isn't       don't

*An apostrophe looks a little like a flying comma. An apostrophe of contraction shows us that letters have been left out.*

a  I will _____      b  it is _____

c  he is _____      d  I am _____

e  is not _____

**2** Write apostrophes of contraction where they belong in the following words.

a  Ill _____   b  hell _____   c  arent _____   d  shed _____

e  whats _____   f  couldnt _____   g  Ive _____   h  were _____

**3** Shorten these words by writing an apostrophe where the missing letters should go. For example: *I have = I've* (The apostrophe takes the place of *h* and *a*.)

a  I am = _____          b  can not = _____

c  I will = _____          d  did not = _____

e  do not = _____          f  we are = _____

g  is not = _____          h  does not = _____

**4** Rewrite these sentences changing the bold words into contractions with apostrophes.

a  **We have** got a new swimming pool in our backyard.

_____

b  **It is** funny how puppies know how we feel.

_____

**TAKE THE CHALLENGE**

Here are some less common contractions. Can you find out what they were before they were shortened?

'tis _____          o'er _____

# Are bunyips real?

Aboriginal stories tell of a terrible creature. It lives in swamps, creeks, waterholes, rivers, lakes and billabongs. The creature is a bunyip.

The stories tell us that the bunyip has a head like a dog and instead of arms, it has flippers. Some say the bunyip is hairy. Others say that it has a long neck with a mane of feathers. All the stories tell us that the bunyip has a frightening roar.

On a clear moonlit night, if you are camping near a waterhole, do not disturb the water when you go to fill up your billycan. If you do, you will annoy any bunyips that are sleeping there. It is said that there is nothing worse than an angry bunyip.

Perhaps bunyips are not real. Perhaps stories of bunyips are told to frighten young children like you into behaving well. What do you think? Are bunyips real?

**1** After each sentence write *S* if it is a statement, write *Q* if it is a question and write *E* if it is an exclamation.

a   Are bunyips real? _____

b   Look out, the bunyip is coming! _____

c   Have you ever seen a bunyip? _____

d   Some say the bunyip is hairy. _____

**2** Write the commas where they correctly belong in these sentences.

a   The bunyip lives in swamps creeks waterholes rivers lakes and billabongs.

b   On our recent trip we passed through Wangaratta Albury Gundagai Yass and Goulburn.

c   Bunyips dragons fairies and goblins are all mysterious creatures.

**3** Rewrite these sentences so that the contraction is written in full.

For example:  You'd better be quiet when filling your billycan.

*You had better be quiet when filling your billy can.*

a   Don't disturb the water. _____

_____

b   It's said that there's nothing worse than an angry bunyip. _____

_____

c   If you disturb the water you'll annoy any bunyips sleeping in the waterhole.

_____

_____

**TAKE THE CHALLENGE**

In your own words, answer the two questions at the end of the story on page 80.

_____

_____

## Sentences and punctuation

**1** Shade the bubble next to the sentence that has the correct punctuation.

○ sam and rupert were walking up jackson street when they saw molly

○ Sam and rupert were walking up jackson street when they saw molly.

○ Sam and Rupert were walking up Jackson Street when they saw Molly.

○ Sam and rupert were walking up Jackson street when they saw molly.

**2** Shade the bubble with the word that should begin with a capital letter.

○ school      ○ saturday      ○ happy      ○ today

**3** Shade the bubble next to the sentence that has the correct punctuation.

○ on friday i went to the cinema and watched *born to ride*

○ On Friday i went to the cinema and watched *Born to Ride*.

○ On Friday I Went to the Cinema and Watched *Born to Ride*.

○ On Friday I went to the cinema and watched *Born to Ride*.

**4** Shade the bubble next to the punctuation mark that is missing from this sentence.

*Did you see how big the moon was last night*

○ .      ○ ?      ○ !      ○ ,

**5** Shade the bubble next to the punctuation mark that is missing from this sentence.

*The flowers in the garden were all in bloom*

○ .      ○ ?      ○ !      ○ ,

**6** Shade the bubble next to the punctuation mark that is missing from this sentence.

*Watch out Lockie*

○ .      ○ ?      ○ !      ○ ,

**7** Shade the bubble next to the sentence that has the correct punctuation.

○ At the aquarium we saw angelfish, jellyfish, sharks and an octopus.

○ At the aquarium we saw angelfish, jellyfish, sharks, and, an octopus.

○ At the aquarium, we saw angelfish, jellyfish, sharks, and an octopus.

○ At the aquarium we saw angelfish jellyfish sharks and an octopus,

**8** Shade the bubble next to the sentence that has the correct punctuation.

○ Sitting on a large red toadstool was a strange little old elf.

○ Sitting, on a large red toadstool, was a strange little old elf.

○ Sitting on a large, red, toadstool, was a strange, little, old elf.

○ Sitting on a large, red toadstool was a strange, little, old elf.

**9** Shade the bubble next to the word with the apostrophe in the correct place.

○ could'nt        ○ coul'dnt        ○ couldn't        ○ couldnt'

**10** Shade the bubble next to the contraction for **she will**.

○ shell        ○ shel'l        ○ sh'ell        ○ she'll

**HOW AM I DOING?**

Colour the boxes if you understand.

Capital letters begin sentences. ☐          Capital letters begin proper nouns. ☐

**I** is always written as a capital letter. ☐        Statements end with full stops. ☐

Questions end with question marks. ☐

Exclamations end with exclamation marks. ☐

Commas can be used to separate nouns or adjectives in a list. ☐

An apostrophe of contraction shows that a letter or letters have been left out. ☐

## UNIT 6.1
### Using grammar in informative texts (information report)

# Gangurrus, kangaroos

Kangaroos are one of Australia's most famous animals. All kangaroos are marsupials called macropods, meaning 'large foot'. A marsupial is a mammal that carries its baby in a pouch.

FACT FILE

Kangaroos are found in every state and territory in Australia. Their habitats range from warm, tropical rainforests and deserts to the colder climates of the southern states.

FACT FILE

Kangaroos have powerful back legs to help them hop and they use their strong tail to help them balance. Kangaroos can hop for long distances at a time.

FACT FILE

Baby kangaroos are born all year round. Soon after birth, the baby kangaroo, called a joey, climbs into its mother's pouch. Joeys feed and grow in this pouch for nine months.

FACT FILE

joey

pouch       large feet

powerful tail

The word 'kangaroo' comes from the Aboriginal word 'gangurru', which is a word in the language of the Guugu Yimithirr people whose traditional land is in Far North Queensland.

FACT FILE

Kangaroos are herbivores. They eat plants such as grass and leaves.

FACT FILE

OXFORD UNIVERSITY PRESS

Information reports are usually written in paragraphs, sometimes with a subheading for each one, to organise bundles of information. The first paragraph is used to introduce or classify the subject. The paragraphs that follow often start with a topic sentence to introduce the main idea of the paragraph.

**1** Read 'Gangurrus, kangaroos'. Highlight the topic sentence at the start of each paragraph, then, using the subheadings below, label each paragraph in the report.

How kangaroos move     How they got their name     A famous marsupial

Baby kangaroos     What they eat     Where they live

Simple sentences are often used in information reports to state facts. For example: *Kangaroos are herbivores.*
Compound sentences, using coordinating conjunctions, are often used to compare details.

**2** Write your own simple sentence to write another fact you know about kangaroos.

_____

**3** Read the paragraph that describes how kangaroos move. Write the compound sentence in this paragraph, then circle the coordinating conjunction.

_____

_____

Information reports are usually written in the present tense, using doing verbs and relating verbs (being and having verbs).

**4** Circle the correct present tense relating verb to complete each sentence below.

a   Female kangaroos **has / have** pouches.

b   A kangaroo **is / are** a powerful animal.

c   There **is / are** different types of kangaroos.

d   That kangaroo **has / have** a baby joey.

**TAKE THE CHALLENGE**

On a piece of paper, write your own paragraph to describe what a kangaroo looks like. Include at least two adjectives.

# Big, bad Barnaby Batteram

Captain Barnaby Batteram <u>was</u> a big, bad, mean pirate with a scar on his face and a patch over his left eye. Together with his loyal crew, he <u>had been plundering</u> the seven seas for many, many years, stealing gold and jewels and burying the precious treasure in secret caves along rugged cliffs and deserted beaches.

However, not only <u>was</u> Captain Barnaby big and bad and mean, he also <u>had</u> a very bad memory. On some days, Barmy, as his crew <u>called</u> him, <u>forgot</u> over which eye he usually <u>wore</u> his patch. On these days, the crew just <u>smiled</u> and <u>continued</u> 'shivering their timbers'.

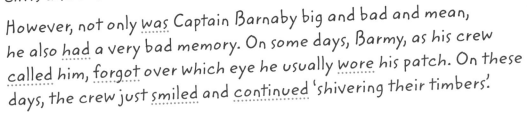

This is so embarrassing.

On other days, Barmy <u>forgot</u> how to make his prisoners walk the plank. His crew just <u>smiled</u> and <u>said</u>, "Oh well, me hearties" and <u>carried on</u> swabbing the decks.

Sometimes this fearsome but forgetful pirate <u>forgot</u> how close his ship <u>needed</u> to be for boarding the rich galleons he <u>wanted to plunder</u> and rob.

When this <u>happened</u>, Barmy's crew <u>pretended</u> they <u>didn't</u> know him. They just <u>looked</u> the other way, all embarrassed.

Follow me lads. Aaghhhh!

Unfortunately, the most worrying thing that Captain Barnaby Batteram often <u>forgot was</u> where he <u>had</u> buried the pirates' treasure chest. When this <u>happened</u>, his crew gave him a very severe look. Sometimes they <u>wouldn't</u> talk to Barmy for the rest of the day!

Imaginative narratives, such as the one about Captain Barnaby Batteram, start with an orientation paragraph. Phrases and adjectives are used to describe the characters and set the scene to tell us where and when this story has taken place.

**1** Read the story of 'Big, bad Barnaby Batteram'. Write the adjectives the author has used in the orientation paragraph to introduce the characters and set the scene.

    **a** *Main character, Captain Barnaby Batteram:* _____

    **b** *Other characters – his crew:* _____

    **c** *Where?* _____ seas, _____ caves,

    _____ cliffs, _____ beaches

    **d** *When?* For _____ years

**2** Use a phrase to add details to these sentences.

    **a** Captain Barmy wore a patch _____.

    **b** He was a mean pirate with a scar _____.

In the second paragraph of the story, the main character has a problem. The author uses adjectives to show how the main character has changed.

**3** Choose adjectives from the box to complete each noun group below – one noun group for a strong character, the other for a weak character.

    big     forgetful     older     fearsome     mean     little

    **a** *Strong character:* a _____ pirate

    **b** *Weak character:* a _____ man

**4** Find an antonym from the story for each word below.

    **a** small _____     **b** good _____

**TAKE THE CHALLENGE**

Look at the underlined verbs on page 86. The author has written this story in the past tense to show that it has already happened. With a partner, take turns reading each paragraph as if it is happening now, in the present tense. Write three examples of present tense verbs you used.

_____    _____    _____

# Homework – good or bad?

Homework is bad! It is bad because it is a waste of time. When children come home from school they are tired. They should be allowed to relax and play computer games, watch TV or play sport.

Children spend six hours a day, five days a week learning at school. Doing school work at home is not fair!

Of course we need to learn, but doing school work at home is not the only way to learn.

Ben E. (Year 3)

I love doing homework!

When I get home from school, I have a snack and a drink and then Mum and I sit down at my table and do my homework together. It is a great way for us to spend some time together. If I get stuck, Mum is there to help me out!

Once I finish my homework, I can go out to play or watch television.

I know that doing my homework will help me with my other school work, so I think homework is good.

Elly B. (Year 3)

Persuasive texts are used to convince readers of something. Persuasive texts often use exclamations to make a point or show strong feelings.

**1** Read the two persuasive texts on page 88.

  **a** Write the two exclamations Ben uses in his text.

  _____

  _____

  **b** Write the two exclamations Elly uses in her text.

  _____

  _____

Persuasive texts or arguments are usually written in the present tense. They often use thinking and feeling verbs to give opinions and modal verbs to tell about the certainty of something happening.

**2** Use verbs in the present tense to complete these argument statements.

  **a** "When children come home from school they _____," said Ben.

  **b** "Mum and I _____ time together," said Elly.

  **c** "When I _____ my homework, I can go out to play," said Elly.

**3** Circle the thinking and feeling verbs in these sentences.

  **a** I love doing my homework.

  **b** Ben considers homework to be a bad thing.

  **c** We prefer to go out and play than do homework.

**4** Find modal verbs on page 88 to complete the sentences.

  **a** Doing my homework _____ help me with my other school work.

  **b** Children _____ be allowed to relax and play computer games.

**TAKE THE CHALLENGE**

Which of the two sentences below makes a stronger argument by including an adverb?

  ☐  I believe homework is good for you.

  ☐  I truly believe homework is good for you.

# Doctor! Doctor!

Doctor Brown! Doctor Brown! I keep thinking that I'm a strawberry.

Dear me, Kevin. You really are in a jam, aren't you?

Doctor Black: What seems to be the trouble?

Maree: I swallowed a clock last week.

Doctor Black: My goodness, why didn't you come sooner?

Maree: I didn't want to alarm anybody.

"Doctor, Doctor, you must help me," said Paul. "I can't remember anything."

"How long has this been going on?" asked Doctor Green.

"How long has what been going on?" said Paul.

Dr Yellow: Zoe, how did you get here so fast?

Zoe: Flu.

"Doctor Red, I've got beans growing out of my ears," cried Jan.

"Oh dear," said Doctor Red. "How did that happen?"

"I've no idea," said Jan. "I planted onions."

Doctor Blue! Doctor Blue! I feel like a pack of cards.

Just sit there, Jenny, and I'll deal with you later.

We can show that someone is speaking and we can show the words that are being spoken in a number of ways. Quoted (direct) speech is the term that refers to words that are actually spoken.

Quoted (direct) speech is sometimes written in a speech bubble or it can be written inside speech marks (quotation marks).

1 Read 'Doctor! Doctor!' and look at the words inside the speech bubbles. Write the words being spoken by:

a  Kevin: _____

b  Doctor Brown: _____

c  Dr Blue: _____

2 Another way to show spoken words is to write them in the form of a play. Write some words spoken by:

a  Dr Black: _____

b  Maree: _____

c  Doctor Yellow: _____

3 Another way to show spoken words in your writing is to use speech marks (quotation marks). For example: *"Help me!" yelled Rex.* What did Rex say? *Help me!*

Write some words spoken by:

a  Paul: "_____"

b  Dr Green: "_____"

c  Jan: "_____"

4 Use quoted (direct) speech to finish this famous conversation.

"Oh my, my, Grandma. What big eyes you have," said Little Red Riding Hood.

"All the better to see you with, my dear," said the Big Bad Wolf.

"Oh my, my, Grandma. What big ears you have," said Little Red Riding Hood.

"_____," said the Big Bad Wolf.

"_____," said Little Red Riding Hood.

_____

**TAKE THE CHALLENGE**

On a piece of paper, write out a 'Knock, knock' joke as if spoken by you and your best friend. Remember to show who is saying what.

# The building Ogs

OXFORD UNIVERSITY PRESS

The word **preposition** means 'placed in front of'. Prepositions are usually placed *in front of* nouns and pronouns to form **prepositional phrases**. For example: *up the ladder, with her*

**1** Look at the picture on page 92. Use **prepositions** from the box to form **prepositional phrases** telling where you will find each Og. Some prepositions may be used more than once.

a   Og A is standing _____ a ladder.

b   Og B is _____ the can of paint.

c   Og D is leaning _____ the edge.

d   Og F is _____ top of the roof.

e   Og G will land _____ a sharp nail.

f   Og H is sliding _____ the roof.

g   Og J is _____ the water tank.

h   Ogs L and N are carrying a plank _____ their shoulders.

i   Og M is _____ the plank.

j   Og O is walking _____ the door.

k   Og P is _____ the wheelbarrow.

l   Og S will be covered _____ sand.

m   Og R is hanging _____ the roof.

off
in
down
on
under
by
from
above
over
with
through
behind

**2** Write your own sentences using these **prepositions**.

a   in _____

b   off _____

c   at _____

**TAKE THE CHALLENGE**

Use the picture on page 92 and the following Ogs and **prepositions** to write your own sentences.

Og I = under _____

Og C = in _____

Og B = against _____

# Hommy Nym juggles!

OXFORD UNIVERSITY PRESS

Homonyms are words that look and/or sound the same.

For example: *Wind the window out and let the wind in please.*

Most homonyms look different but sound the same. These homonyms are called homophones.

For example: *cheap* (not expensive); *cheep* (a bird's call)

**1** Match the homophones in the box with the things that Hommy Nym juggles.

For example: *Hommy juggles a hoarse horse, a stake in a steak, etc.*

| hoarse | tale | son | leek | leak | horse | tail |
| deer | steak | sun | dear | stake | pear | pair |

Hommy juggles _____

_____

_____

> Words that sound the same but are spelled differently and have different meanings are called homophones.

**2** Match the homophones in the box with their meanings.

| week weak male mail ball bawl see sea steel steal one won |

a    a man or boy _____

b    look at _____

c    not strong _____

d    cry loudly _____

e    a single thing _____

f    seven days _____

g    a metal _____

h    salty water _____

i    letters and parcels _____

j    the past of *win* _____

k    take something that belongs to someone else _____

l    a round or egg-shaped bouncy thing _____

**3** Circle the correct homophone to match the picture.

flower/flour           meet/meat           sent/cent/scent

poor/pour           sell/cell           creek/creak

**TAKE THE CHALLENGE**

On a piece of paper, draw one of the following:

- a ewe chasing you
- a knight at night
- a mayor on a mare
- a male delivering mail
- someone with a board who is bored

# Ridiculous rhymes

Careless Connie climbed a ladder
her aim to reach the top,
But Careless Connie was not careful —
she forgot to stop!

Ollie bought a magic kit
and practised for a year.
Now Ollie's finally mastered it
and made Ollie disappear.

"Please be helpful," said my dad
"and go outside to play."
"But Dad we're in a submarine
on the bottom of the bay!"

AjW

A prefix comes at the beginning of a word. A prefix changes the meaning of a word.

**1** Add one of the prefixes from the box to change the meanings of these words to opposites. The prefixes can be used more than once.

a _____ fair

b _____ appear

c _____ lock

d _____ possible

e _____ visible

f _____ behave

g _____ respect

h _____ perfect

dis-

un-

im-

in-

mis-

A suffix comes at the end of a word. A suffix also changes the meaning of a word.

**2** Add the suffixes -ful and -less to write each of these words as antonyms (opposites).
For example: use = useful, useless

a care _____ _____

b rest _____ _____

c help _____ _____

d colour _____ _____

e power _____ _____

**TAKE THE CHALLENGE**

Add prefixes or change the suffixes of these words to make them opposites.

a possible _____

b obey _____

c merciful _____

d fearless _____

# WHO SAID THAT?

1. "Who's been eating my porridge?" said Papa Bear.

2. "I'll huff and I'll puff and I'll blow your house down!" shouted the Wolf.

3. "Why Grandma, what big eyes you have," said the little girl.

4. "Run, run as fast as you can. You can't catch me!" teased the tiny fellow.

5. "I had a terrible night's sleep," she moaned. "There was a lump in all those mattresses."

6. "Sorry Prince," the beautiful girl gasped, "it's right on midnight and I have to leave right now!"

7. "Hey Jack!" called the seller. "Would you like to trade your cow for a few beans?"

8. "Mirror, Mirror on the wall, who is the fairest of them all?" asked the Queen.

OXFORD UNIVERSITY PRESS

**1** Use the **direct speech** on page 98 to help you answer these questions.

a   Who was talking to Jack? _____

b   Who asked a question about porridge? _____

c   Why did someone have a bad night's sleep? _____

_____

d   Who is saying something threatening? _____

e   Who was the beautiful girl talking to? _____

**2** Write the actual words spoken by these characters on page 98.

a   The Queen _____

_____

_____

b   the little girl _____

_____

_____

c   the seller _____

_____

_____

**TAKE THE CHALLENGE**

Write numbers to match these fairy tales with the **direct speech** on page 98.

The Gingerbread Man _____   Little Red Riding Hood _____

Goldilocks and the Three Bears _____   The Princess and the Pea _____

Jack and the Beanstalk _____   Cinderella _____

The Three Little Pigs _____   Snow White and the Seven Dwarfs _____

# TOPICS 6 AND 7: TEST YOUR GRAMMAR!

## Using grammar

**1** Shade the bubble that shows the correct direct speech for the cartoon.

"What do bees do with their honey?"
"They cell it."

- ○ What do bees do with their honey asked Mika. They cell it answered Trin.
- ○ Mika asked what bees do with their honey and Trin said they cell it.
- ○ "What do bees do with their honey?" asked Mika. "They cell it," answered Trin.
- ○ What do bees do with their honey, "asked Mika?" They cell it, "answered Trin."

**2** Shade the bubble that shows the homophone from the cartoon above.

- ○ cell
- ○ do
- ○ honey
- ○ with

**3** Shade the bubble that shows the preposition in this phrase.

*under the shady tree*

- ○ under
- ○ the
- ○ shady
- ○ tree

**4** Shade the bubble that shows a sentence with a prepositional phrase.

- ○ "Look out!" he shouted.
- ○ I like to eat cheese nibbles.
- ○ He could clearly see a koala in the tree.
- ○ The boy's name was Sayeed.

**5** Shade the bubble that shows the prefix that would make this word an opposite – **agree**.

- ○ un
- ○ im
- ○ mis
- ○ dis

OXFORD UNIVERSITY PRESS

**6** Shade the bubble that shows a word with a suffix.

○ truthful          ○ truth          ○ untruth          ○ true

**7** Shade the bubble with the prefix that would make this word an opposite – **possible**.

○ un          ○ im          ○ mis          ○ dis

**8** Shade the bubble that shows correct direct speech for the following:

*Alice asked the Caterpillar why he was wearing such a funny hat.*

○ Why are you wearing such a funny hat Mr C

○ "Why are you wearing such a funny hat Mr C?" asked Alice.

○ "Alice," asked Mr C "Why he was wearing such a funny hat."

○ "Why are you wearing such a funny hat Mr C asked Alice?"

**HOW AM I DOING?**

Colour the boxes if you understand.

Quoted or direct speech shows the words that are actually spoken. ☐

Prepositional phrases can tell us where something is happening. ☐

Homophones are words that sound the same but look different and have

different meanings. For example: *rode/road, blue/blew* ☐

# TIME TO REFLECT

Colour the box when you can do the things listed.

☐ I can use common nouns and proper nouns.

☐ I choose suitable nouns in my writing to represent different characters. For example: **girl**, **orphan**, **prince**

☐ I can use pronouns to represent people, places and things.

☐ I can use adjectives to describe characters and settings to make my writing more interesting.

☐ I know how to use articles and adjectives to make more interesting noun groups.

☐ I use verbs in every sentence I write.

☐ I use thinking and feeling verbs in my writing.

☐ I use lots of different saying verbs in my writing to show the way someone is talking.

☐ I know how to use relating verbs (being and having verbs) when I am writing facts in descriptions and reports.

☐ I can use present, past and future tense verbs correctly.

☐ I use adverbs to tell more about the verbs in my sentences.

☐ I use modal verbs such as **could, would, should** and **must** when expressing opinions.

☐ I add phrases to my writing to give details such as **where, when, how** or **why** something is happening.

☐ I understand that some words have opposites (antonyms).

☐ I understand that some words have similar meanings (synonyms).

☐ I use paragraphs to organise my writing into logical bundles.

☐ I sometimes use rhythm, alliteration or onomatopoeia to make my imaginative text writing more interesting or playful.

☐ I know how to use the coordinating conjunctions **and, but, or** and **so** to write longer sentences.

☐ I understand that the subject and verb in a sentence must agree.

☐ I use capital letters to begin sentences, to write the pronoun I, and when I write proper nouns.

☐ I use commas in lists and know when to use full stops, question marks and exclamation marks.

☐ I understand that an apostrophe of contraction is used to show where a letter is missing in a shortened word.

# GLOSSARY

| | |
|---|---|
| **adjective** | A describing word: *red, old, large, round, three* |
| **adverb** | A word that adds meaning, usually to a verb, to tell when, where or how something happened: *slowly, immediately, soon, here* |
| **alliteration** | A group of words that begin with or contain the same sound: *seven silly sausages* |
| **antonym** | An opposite: *full/empty, sitting/standing, front/back* |
| **article** | The words *a, an* and *the* |
| **apostrophe of contraction** | A punctuation mark that shows where letters are missing in a shortened word: *isn't, we'll, I'm, shouldn't* |
| **capital letter** | An upper-case letter: *ABCDEFGHIJKLMNOPQRSTUVWXYZ* |
| **comma** | A punctuation mark that shows a short break or pause in a sentence, separates words in a list or separates parts of a sentence. |
| **coordinating conjunction** | A joining word used to join two simple sentences or main ideas: *and, but, or, so* |
| **exclamation** | A sentence that shows a raised voice or strong feeling: *Look out!* |
| **exclamation mark** | The mark (!) that shows where an exclamation ends. |
| **full stop** | The mark that shows where a statement ends: *Zoe is at school.* |
| **homophone** | A word that sounds the same but is spelled differently: *sun/son* |
| **main clause** | A simple sentence or main idea that always contains a subject and a verb and makes sense by itself. |
| **noun** | A word that names people, places, animals, things or ideas. Nouns can be: <br><br> abstract nouns (things that cannot be seen or touched): *happiness* <br> common nouns (names of ordinary things): *hat, toys, pet, mouse, clock, bird* <br> concrete nouns (things that can be seen or touched): *book, pet, boy, girl* <br> proper nouns (special names): *Max, Perth, Friday, March, Grand Final* <br> technical nouns (sometimes called scientific nouns): *oxygen* |
| **noun group** | A group of words, often including an article, an adjective and a noun, built around a main noun: *the strange, old house* |
| **onomatopoeia** | Words that sound like the thing they are describing: *Bang! Crash!* |

| | |
|---|---|
| **paragraph** | A section of text containing a number of sentences about a particular point. Each paragraph starts on a new line. |
| **phrase** | A group of words that adds details about when, where, how, why: *the car, after lunch, with a spoon, for Olivia* |
| **plural** | More than one: *chairs, dishes, boxes, cities, donkeys, loaves, fungi* |
| **preposition** | A word that usually begins a phrase: *on, in, over, under, before* |
| **prepositional phrase** | A phrase that always begins with a preposition: *on the shelf, in the car, over the hill, under the bridge* |
| **pronoun** | A word that can take the place of a noun to represent a person, place or thing: *he, she, I, it, they, we, us, me, they, them, mine* |
| **question** | A sentence that asks something: *Is Tock hiding under the bed?* |
| **quoted (direct) speech** | The words that someone actually says. Quoted speech uses quotation marks at the start and end of the actual words spoken. |
| **sentence** | A group of words that makes sense and includes a subject and at least one verb. |
| | A simple sentence has one main idea and one verb or verb group: *The birds were sitting on the fence.* |
| | A compound sentence uses *and, but, or, so* to join two main ideas. A compound sentence has two verbs or verb groups: *Some birds were sitting on the fence and a cat was lurking below.* |
| **statement** | A sentence that states facts or gives opinions: *The horses ran around the paddock. I like ice cream.* |
| **subject** | The noun or noun group naming who or what a sentence is about. |
| **synonym** | A word that means the same or nearly the same as another word: *shouts/yells, thin/skinny* |
| **topic sentence** | A sentence, usually placed at the start of a paragraph, that introduces the main point being made in the paragraph. |
| **verb** | A word that tells us what is happening in a sentence. Verbs can be: |
| | doing verbs: *walked, swam* <br> saying verbs: *said, asked* <br> thinking and feeling verbs: *know, like* <br> relating verbs: *am, is, are, had* <br> modal verbs (telling how sure we are about doing something): *should, could, would, may, might, must, can, will, shall* |
| **verb group** | A group of words built around a head word that is a verb: *might have been wondering* |
| **verb tense** | The form a verb takes to show when an action takes place – in the present, past or future: *runs/is running, thought/was thinking, will help* |